Dr. Radha Mahendran
Suganya Jeyabaskar
Astral Gabriella Francis

Computational Approaches for Identifying Drugs Against Alzheimer's Disease

Anchor Academic
Publishing

Mahendran, Radha, Jeyabaskar, Suganya, Francis, Astral Gabriella: Computational Approaches for Identifying Drugs Against Alzheimer's Disease, Hamburg, Anchor Academic Publishing 2017

Buch-ISBN: 978-3-96067-138-1
PDF-eBook-ISBN: 978-3-96067-638-6
Druck/Herstellung: Anchor Academic Publishing, Hamburg, 2017

Bibliografische Information der Deutschen Nationalbibliothek:
Die Deutsche Nationalbibliothek verzeichnet diese Publikation in der Deutschen Nationalbibliografie; detaillierte bibliografische Daten sind im Internet über http://dnb.d-nb.de abrufbar.

Bibliographical Information of the German National Library:
The German National Library lists this publication in the German National Bibliography. Detailed bibliographic data can be found at: http://dnb.d-nb.de

© Anchor Academic Publishing, Imprint der Diplomica Verlag GmbH
Hermannstal 119k, 22119 Hamburg
http://www.diplomica-verlag.de, Hamburg 2017
Printed in Germany

PREFACE

Alzheimer's disease is the most common cause of dementia that leads to problems with memory, thinking and behavior. Alzheimer's disease is named after the Scientist Alois Alzheimer, who described it as a physical disease that affects the brain. During the course of the disease, proteins build up in the brain to form structures called plaques. This leads to the loss of connection between the nerve cells and eventually leads to the death of the nerve cells and loss of the brain tissues. People with Alzheimer's also have a shortage of some important chemicals in the brain by which the signals are not transmitted effectively. So far there is no cure for Alzheimer's disease. In this study, 3D QSAR and pharmacophore mapping studies were carried out using Accelrys Discovery Studio 2.1. Quantitative Structure–Activity Relationship models (QSAR models) are classification models used in the chemical and biological sciences. β-Secretase is an important protease in the pathogenesis of Alzheimer's disease. Some statine-based peptidomimetics show inhibitory activities to β-secretase. To explore the inhibitory mechanism, molecular docking and three-dimensional quantitative structure–activity relationship (3D-QSAR) studies on these analogues were performed. This study was useful in identifying the involvement of statine-based peptidomimetics and their analogues in the treatment of Alzheimer's disease. Further in vitro studies could be carried out to find a potent target in curing Alzheimer's disease.

ACKNOWLEDGEMENTS

First and foremost, I thank **God** for enabling me to complete this project.

I would like to express my sincere gratitude to our Management, especially ***Dr.Ishari k.Ganesh, Chancellor, Vels University***, Founder-Chairman, Vels group of Institutions, for giving us a platform to prove ourselves in the field of Bioinformatics and constantly motivating us in all our endeavours.

Dr.A.Jothi Murugan, Vice-President (P&D), Vels University deserves a big word of thanks from me since he was a silent motivator for all our academic achievements.

I would like to thank ***Dr.V. Thamizh Arasan, Vice-Chancellor, Vels University*** for always motivating us.

I would also like to thank ***Dr.S.Sivasubramaniam, Advisor-Research &Development, Vels University*** for always encouraging us.

I record my sincere gratitude to the ***Registrar, Dr. A. R.Veeramani*** and the ***Controller of Examinations***, ***Dr. A. Joseph Durai*** for their support.

I am Very thankful to ***Dr.DinakaranMichael, Dean, School of Life sciences,*** for his constant help and support in all our endeavours.

I thank the editorial team of *publishing*, for taking effort in editing this project and constantly giving their opinions during the course of time.

I wish to express my sincere and warm Acknowledgements to my ***Family members*** for their encouragement and support.

THANKS TO ALL

Dr. Radha Mahendran

DEDICATION

This work is dedicated to my *Guru, Dr.G.JAYARAMAN* (Late) *Professor & co-ordinator, Molecular biology program, Department of Genetics, DR.ALM.PG. Institute of Basic Medical Sciences, Taramani, University of Madras*, Chennai, India.

I thank him for being my *MENTOR, LEADER, INSTRUCTOR, GUIDE AND INSPIRATION.*

Dr. Radha Mahendran

Index

1) Abstract........................ 1

2) Introduction.................... 2

3) Review of Literature............. 8

4) Materials...................... 21

5) Methodology................... 23

6) Results and Discussion.......... 29

7) Conclusion.................... 57

8) Bibliography................... 58

ABSTRACT

Alzheimer's disease is the most common form of dementia which is incurable. Although some kinds of memory loss are normal during aging, the changes due to aging are not severe enough to interfere with the level of function. β-Secretase is an important protease in the pathogenesis of Alzheimer's disease. Some statine-based peptidomimetics show inhibitory activities to β-secretase. To explore the inhibitory mechanism, Molecular docking and three-dimensional quantitative structure–activity relationship (3D-QSAR) studies on these analogues were performed. Quantitative structure-activity relationship (QSAR) modeling pertains to the construction of predictive models of biological activities as a function of structural and molecular information of a compound library. The concept of QSAR has typically been used for drug discovery and development and has gained wide applicability for correlating molecular information with not only biological activities but also with other physicochemical properties, which has therefore been termed quantitative structure-property relationship (QSPR). In this study, 3D QSAR and pharmacophore mapping studies were carried out using Accelrys Discovery Studio 2.1. Nine best drugs were selected out of the 16 ligands and pharmacophore features were generated. Further hypothesis was done using Hypogen and out of 3 molecules selected one molecule produced the highest fit value of 3.473 from the test set. Hence, it could be one of the best drugs in the treatment of Alzheimer's disease.

1

INTRODUCTION

ALZHEIMER'S DISEASE:

Alzheimer's disease is a progressive, degenerative disorder that attacks the brain's nerve cells, or neurons, resulting in loss of memory, thinking and language skills, and behavioral changes. These neurons, which produce the brain chemical, or neurotransmitter, acetylcholine, break connections with other nerve cells and ultimately die. For example, short-term memory fails when Alzheimer's disease first destroys nerve cells in the hippocampus, and language skills and judgment decline when neurons die in the cerebral cortex.

Two types of abnormal lesions clog the brains of individuals with Alzheimer's disease: β-amyloid plaques—sticky clumps of protein fragments and cellular material that form outside and around neurons; and neurofibrillary tangles—insoluble twisted fibers composed largely of the protein tau that build up inside nerve cells. Although these structures are hallmarks of the disease, scientists are unclear whether they cause it or a byproduct of it.

Alzheimer's disease is the most common cause of dementia, or loss of intellectual function, among people aged 65 and older. Alzheimer's disease is not a normal part of aging. Origin of the term Alzheimer's disease dates back to 1906 when Dr. Alois Alzheimer, a German physician, presented a case history before a medical meeting of a 51-year-old woman who suffered from a rare brain disorder. A brain autopsy identified the plaques and tangles that today characterize Alzheimer's disease (1).

Alzheimer's disease, the most common form of dementia in the elderly, is a neurodegenerative disorder that is characterized by a slow but progressive loss of cognitive function. Extracellular amyloid plaques, intracellular neurofibrillary tangles, and loss of neurons and synapses resulting in brain atrophy are the main pathological hallmarks of Alzheimer's disease. Disease onset is usually after the age of 70 years, although the prevalence increases exponentially with age after the age of 65 years and exceeds 25% in those over the age of 90 years (2).

Differential diagnosis of dementing diseases is very important to rule in the so-called treatable dementia. The new DSM-IV criteria for dementia include memory

2

disturbances and one or more of aphasia, apraxia, or frontal lobe dysfunctions as essentials. Alzheimer disease requires, in addition, slowly progressive course and ruling out other brain or systemic diseases. Vascular dementia requires focal neurological or neuroimaging signs. Other diseases which cause dementia include chronic subdural hematoma, infection and brain tumor. CT or MRI can readily diagnose them if suspected and they may be treated. Systemic diseases associated with treatable dementia include electrolyte disturbances, hypothyroidism, vitamin deficiency, alcohol or drug intoxication, syphilis and HIV infection. Prevention of dementia seems to be the future problem as we could prevent cerebrovascular diseases by treating hypertension (3).

DEVELOPMENT OF THE DISEASE:

It is possible to test for the ApoE4 gene, but such a test does not predict whether a particular person will develop Alzheimer's disease or not. It merely indicates that he or she is at greater risk. There are in fact people who have had the ApoE4 gene, lived well into old age and never developed Alzheimer's disease, just as there are people who did not have ApoE4, who did develop the disease. Therefore taking such a test carries the risk of unduly alarming or comforting somebody. Only in very rare families where Alzheimer's disease is a dominant genetic disorder unaffected relatives may take a predictive diagnostic test (4).

STAGES OF THE DISEASE:

Alzheimer's disease typically progresses slowly in three general stages:

- **Mild (early-stage),**
- **Moderate (middle-stage), and**
- **Severe (late-stage).**

Since Alzheimer's affects people in different ways, each person will experience symptoms - or progress through Alzheimer's stages - differently.

Mild Alzheimer's disease (early-stage)

In the early stages of Alzheimer's, a person may function independently. The person may still work and be part of social activities. Despite this, the person may feel having memory lapses, such as forgetting familiar words or the location of everyday objects.

Moderate Alzheimer's disease (middle-stage)

Moderate Alzheimer's is typically the longest stage and can last for many years. As the disease progresses, the person with Alzheimer's will require a greater level of care.

Severe Alzheimer's disease (late-stage)

In the final stage of this disease, individuals lose the ability to respond to their environment, to carry on a conversation and, eventually, to control movement. They may still say words or phrases, but communicating pain becomes difficult. As memory and cognitive skills continue to worsen, personality changes may take place and individuals need extensive help with daily activities (5).

CAUSES OF THE DISEASE:

The diagnosis of dementia is intended to encompass the spectrum of severity, ranging from the mildest to the most severe stages of dementia. The methodology for staging of dementia severity was beyond the charge of the workgroup. Dementia is diagnosed when there are cognitive or behavioral (neuropsychiatric) symptoms that:

- Interfere with the ability to function at work or at usual activities;
- Represent a decline from previous levels of functioning and performing;
- Are not explained by delirium or major psychiatric disorder;
- Cognitive impairment is detected and diagnosed through a combination of (1) history-taking from the patient and a knowledgeable informant and (2) an objective cognitive assessment, mental status examination or neuropsychological testing. Neuropsychological testing should be performed when the routine history and bedside mental status examination cannot provide a confident diagnosis.
- The cognitive or behavioral impairment involves a minimum of two of the following domains:

   a. Impaired ability to acquire and remember new information—symptoms include: repetitive questions or conversations, misplacing personal belongings, forgetting events or appointments, getting lost on a familiar route.

   b. Impaired reasoning and handling of complex tasks, poor judgment—symptoms include: poor understanding of safety risks, inability to manage finances, poor decision-making ability, inability to plan complex or sequential activities.

4

c. Impaired visuospatial abilities—symptoms include: inability to recognize faces or common objects or to find objects in direct view despite good acuity, inability to operate simple implements, or orient clothing to the body.

d. Impaired language functions (speaking, reading, writing)—symptoms include: difficulty thinking of common words while speaking, hesitations; speech, spelling, and writing errors.

e. Changes in personality, behavior, or comportment—symptoms include: uncharacteristic mood fluctuations such as agitation, impaired motivation, initiative, apathy, loss of drive, social withdrawal, decreased interest in previous activities, loss of empathy, compulsive or obsessive behaviors, socially unacceptable behaviors.

The differentiation of dementia from MCI rests on the determination of whether or not there is significant interference in the ability to function at work or in usual daily activities. This is inherently a clinical judgment made by a skilled clinician on the basis of the individual circumstances of the patient and the description of daily affairs of the patient obtained from the patient *and* from a knowledgeable informant (6).

SYMPTOMS OF THE DISEASE:

Alzheimer's disease symptoms vary among individuals. The most common initial symptom is a gradually worsening ability to remember new information. This occurs because the first neurons to be damaged and destroyed are usually in brain regions involved in forming new memories. As neurons in other parts of the brain are damaged and destroyed, individuals experience other difficulties. The following are common symptoms of Alzheimer's: Memory loss that disrupts daily life; Challenges in planning or solving problems; Difficulty completing familiar tasks at home, at work or at leisure; Confusion with time or place; Trouble understanding visual images and spatial relationships; Misplacing things and losing the ability to retrace steps; Decreased or poor judgment; Withdrawal from work or social activities; Changes in mood and personality, including apathy and depression; Increased anxiety, agitation and sleep disturbances.

5

DIAGNOSIS AND DIAGNOSTIC CRITERIA:

No single, simple test exists to diagnose Alzheimer's disease. Instead, one's physician, often with the help of a neurologist, will use a variety of approaches and tools to help make a diagnosis. They include the following:

- Obtaining a medical and family history from the individual, including psychiatric history and history of cognitive and behavioral changes.
- Asking a family member or other person close to the individual to provide input about changes in thinking skills or behavior.
- Conducting cognitive tests and physical and neurologic examinations.
- Having the individual undergo blood tests and brain imaging to rule out other potential causes of dementia symptoms, such as a tumor or certain vitamin deficiencies.

Diagnosing Alzheimer's requires a careful and comprehensive medical evaluation. Although physicians can almost always determine if a person has dementia, it may be difficult to identify the exact cause. Several days or weeks may be needed for the patient to complete the required tests and examinations and for the physician to interpret the results and make a diagnosis (7).

PREVENTION:

Two main trends have dominated prevention research so far: first, most studies have focused on preventing dementia, the most severe stage of late-life cognitive impairment, rather than on preventing milder, more common forms of cognitive impairment; secondly, AD dominates dementia prevention research, with less attention given to preventing cognitive impairment of mixed or non-Alzheimer's causes. Such trends are direct consequences of how the criteria for AD were formulated three decades ago: (i) no specific diagnosis is available until the dementia stage; (ii) the diagnosis must be established in two steps, first the dementia syndrome, then the underlying disease; (iii) the dementia syndrome relies heavily on memory impairment, the main feature of AD; and (iv) AD is a diagnosis of exclusion, established when dementia is not due to other brain pathologies (8).

TREATMENT:

Acetylcholinesterase (AChE) inhibitors are an important class of medicinal agents used for the treatment of Alzheimer's disease (9). In order to identify the essential structural features and physicochemical properties for acetylcholinesterase (AChE) inhibitory activity in some carbamate derivatives, the systematic QSAR (Quantitative Structure Activity Relationship) studies (CoMFA, advance CoMFA and CoMSIA) have been carried out.

These studies may provide important insights into structural variations leading to the development of novel AChE inhibitors which may be useful in the development of novel molecules for the treatment of Alzheimer's disease (10).

There are no drug treatments that can cure Alzheimer's disease or any other common type of dementia. However, medicines have been developed for Alzheimer's disease that can temporarily alleviate symptoms, or slow down their progression, in some people. This factsheet explains how the main drug treatments for Alzheimer's disease work, how to access them, and when they can be prescribed and used effectively (11).

Mild cognitive impairment (MCI) was treated in the past as a transitional state between the physiological aging and dementia. Currently it is a separate diagnosis, although very heterogeneous. It requires clinical vigilance because of possibility of conversion to dementia, most often to Alzheimer's disease (AD), with an average of 7-15% per year. The moment of conversion is very important due to the possibility of therapeutic effects, which are most effective in the early stages of AD, while the recommended treatment of MCI does not exist. Criteria for diagnosis of AD (NIA/AA, 2011) include not only the dementia phase but also the MCI phase and preclinical phase of Alzheimer's disease pathophysiological process, when pathological changes are present in the brain but the patient does not have any clinical symptoms. Such state can last for even twenty years (12).

REVIEW OF LITERATURE

QSAR:

The Quantitative Structure Activity Relationship (QSAR) paradigm is based on the assumption that there is an underlying relationship between the molecular structure and biological activity. On this assumption QSAR attempts to establish a correlation between various molecular properties of a set of molecules with their experimentally known biological activity. There are two main objectives for the development of QSAR: A) Development of predictive and robust QSAR, with a specified chemical domain, for prediction of activity of untested molecules. B) It acts as an informative tool by extracting significant patterns in descriptors related to the measured biological activity leading to understanding of mechanisms of given biological activity. This could help in suggesting a design of novel molecules with improved activity profile (13).

QSAR AND ITS RELEVANCE WITH DRUG DISCOVERY:

The concept of quantitative SAR (QSAR) is inherently imbued with an expectation of predictivity, novel insights and the generation of useful hypotheses, particularly as applied to the drug discovery process. However, even recently developed QSAR models often appear to be flawed, characterized by mediocre predictive power and undecipherable descriptors. As a result, users may be able to derive only a vague notion of which molecular features are correlated to activity. Consideration of several precautions is necessary to attempt to circumvent the misuse and misunderstanding of the QSAR technique. Issues related with QSAR include an erroneous association of correlation with causation, the close relationship between large numbers of descriptors and the effect of chance factor, the misuse of the 'leave-one-out' paradigm, and finally, the QSAR enigma, wherein the predictivity of a model is not necessarily a measure of a model's utility.

IMPORTANCE IN DRUG RESEARCH:

One of the important objectives of QSAR is to get useful information for the synthesis of more active or less toxic compounds. QSAR has correctly predicted the activity of large number of compounds before their synthesis (14).

8

MOLECULAR DESCRIPTORS:

Molecular descriptors are terms that characterize specific information about a studied molecule. They are the "numerical values associated with the chemical constitution for correlation of chemical structures with various physical properties, chemical reactivity or biological activity. The modeled response is represented as a function of quantitative values of structural features or properties that are termed as descriptors for a QSAR model. Cheminformatics methods depend on the generation of chemical reference spaces into which new chemical entities are predictable by the developed QSAR model. The definition of chemical spaces significantly depends on the use of computational descriptors of studied molecular structure, physical or chemical properties, or specific features.

The type of descriptors used and the extent to which they can encode the structural features of the molecules that are correlated to the response are critical determinants of the quality of any QSAR model. The descriptors may be physicochemical (hydrophobic, steric or electronic), structural (based on the frequency of occurrence of a substructure), topological electronic (based on molecular orbital calculations), geometric (based on a molecular surface area calculation) (15). Molecular descriptors can be defined as a numerical representation of chemical information encoded within a molecular structure via mathematical procedure. Type of QSAR is based on the dimensionality of molecular descriptors used : 0D - These are descriptors derived from molecular formula e.g. molecular weight, number and type of atoms etc. **1D** - A substructure list representation of a molecule can be considered as a one-dimensional (1D) molecular representation and consists of a list of molecular fragments (e.g. functional groups, rings, bonds, substituents etc.). **2D** - A molecular graph contains topological or two dimensional (2D) information. It describes how the atoms are bonded in a molecule, both the type of bonding and the interaction of particular atoms (e.g. total path count, molecular connectivity indices etc.). **3D** - These are calculated starting from a geometrical or 3D representation of a molecule. These descriptors include molecular surface, molecular volume and other geometrical properties. There are different types of 3D descriptors e.g. electronic, steric, shape etc. **4D** - In addition to the 3D descriptors the 4th dimension is generally in terms of different conformations or any other experimental condition (13).

9

ADVANTAGES OF QSAR:

1. QSAR is important in drug development as it provide quantitative information relating properties of a compound to its activity.

2. QSAR provides a cost effective means of modifying drug molecules by in silico design and enhancement.

3. It quantifies the relationship between structure and activity which provides an understanding of the effect of structure on activity.

4. There is also the potential of make predictions leading to the synthesis of novel analogues.

5. Care must be taken not to use extrapolation outside the range of the data set.

6. The result of QSAR can be used to help understanding interactions between functional groups in the molecules of greatest activity with those of their target (16).

TYPES OF QSAR:

Many QSAR models have been developed and the degree of adequacy of molecular structure varies. The different types of QSAR are given below:

1D models conside only the gross formula of molecule. Such molecules reflect only a comparison of the molecule. Obviously, it is quite impossible to solve adequately the "structure-activity" tasks using such approaches. These models usually have an auxillary role only, but sometimes they can be used as independent virtual screening tools.

2D models contain information regarding the structure and compound and are based on its structural formula. Such models reflect only the topology of the molecule. These models are very popular. The capacity of such approaches is due to the fact that the topological models of molecular structure, in an implicit form, contain information about possible conformations of the compound.

3D QSAR models give full structural information taking into account the topology, composition and spatial shape of the molecule for one conformer only. These molecules are widespread. However, the choice of the conformer of the molecule is analyzed (17).

VARIETY OF APPLICATIONS OF QSAR:

The ability to predict a biological activity is valuable in any number of industries. Whilst some QSARs appear to be little more than academic studies, there are a large number of applications of these models within industries, academia and governmental (regulatory) agencies. A small number of potential uses are listed below:

- The rational identification of new leads within pharmacological, biocidal or pesticidal activity.
- The optimization of pharmacological, biocidal or pesticidal activity.
- The rational design of various other products such as surface-active agents, perfumes, dyes and fine chemicals.
- The identification of hazardous compounds at early stages of product development or the screening of inventories of existing compounds.
- The designing out of toxicity and side-effects in new compounds.
- The prediction of toxicity to humans through deliberate, occasional and occupational exposure.
- The prediction of toxicity to environmental species.
- The selection of compounds with optimal pharmacokinetic properties, whether it be stability or availability in biological systems (18).

LIMITATIONS:

1. Measuring the biological activity in accurate.
2. For listing the biological acting large animal using.
3. Difficult to express 3 D component in term of physic – chemical properties.
4. Chiral drug study may be difficult (19).

β-SECRETASE:

β-Secretase (memapsin 2; BACE1) is the first protease in the processing of amyloid precursor protein leading to the production of amyloid-β (Aβ) in the brain. It is believed that high levels of brain Aβ are responsible for the pathogenesis of Alzheimer's disease (AD). Therefore, β-secretase is a major therapeutic target for the development of inhibitor drugs. During the past decade, steady progress has been made in the evolution of β-secretase inhibitors toward better drug properties. Recent inhibitors are potent, selective and have been shown to penetrate the blood-brain barrier to inhibit Aβ level in the brains of experimental animals. A small number of β-secretase inhibitors have also entered early phase clinical trials. These developments offer some optimism for the clinical development of a disease-modifying drug for AD (20).

The proteinase originally termed 'β-secretase', catalyses the initial step in the amyloidogenic metabolism of the large transmembrane amyloid precursor protein (APP), releasing a soluble APPβ (sAPPβ) ectodomain and simultaneously generating a membrane-bound, C-terminal fragment consisting of 99 amino acids (CTF99). The latter is then further processed by the γ-secretase enzyme complex which, in turn, generates the APP intracellular domain and releases the 39–42-amino-acid amyloid β-peptide (Aβ). An alternative and protective ('non-amyloidogenic') pathway of APP metabolism is initiated by the metalloproteinase, α-secretase pathway, which predominates in most cell types. The identification of the Aβ peptide as the main constituent of the extracellular plaques which characterize Alzheimer's disease (AD) led to the formulation of the 'amyloid cascade' hypothesis of AD. Interruption of this metabolic cascade at one of several sites could potentially reduce the amyloid burden, and slow or even reverse the devastating consequences of the disease. Hence, the identification of β-secretase and the formulation of potent and selective inhibitors of the enzyme that can cross the blood–brain barrier have been the primary targets of pharmaceutical development for almost two decades. β-Secretase is particularly attractive in this context, as it catalyses the first and rate-limiting step in the pathway. Its deletion in mice has minimal phenotypic and behavioral consequences, although more recent data have suggested subtle phenotypic changes in β-secretase-deficient mice, and the enzyme appears to play a role in both peripheral and central myelination.

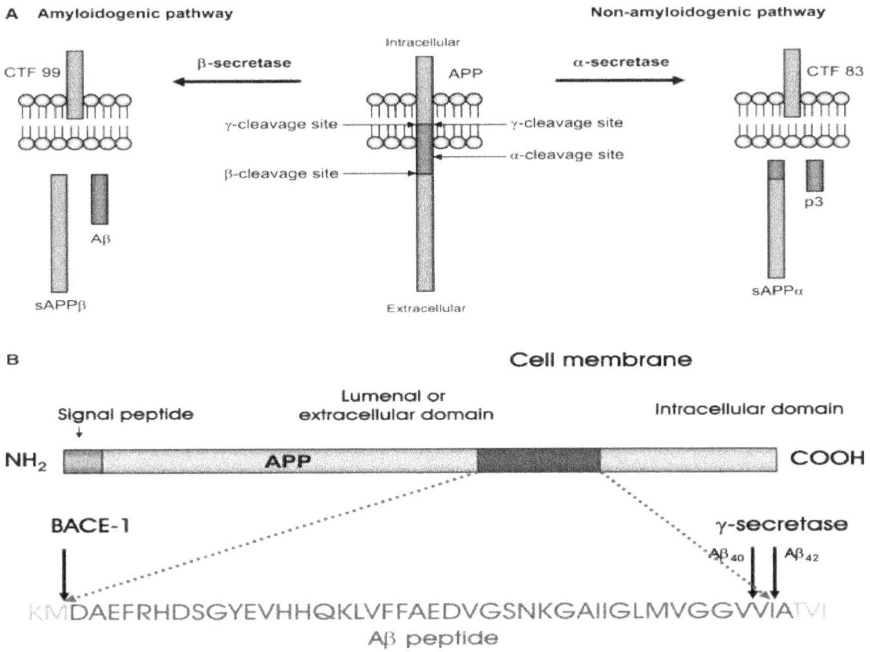

Fig. 1: Processing of APP to form Aβ peptides (Ref: 21)

(A) Schematic diagram of the alternative processing pathways of APP. The transmembrane APP undergoes two alternative and competing pathways of metabolism. The major and non-amyloidogenic, or α-secretase, pathway precludes the formation of Alzheimer's Aβ peptide. The amyloidogenic, or β-secretase, pathway initiates the formation of Aβ, which is completed by the action of the γ-secretase. α-Secretase has been identified as a zinc metalloproteinase of the ADAMs family, whereas both β- and γ-secretases are membrane-bound aspartic.

(B) Sites of cleavage of APP by β- and γ-secretases to form Aβ peptides. The sites of the juxtamembrane and intramembrane cleavages of transmembrane APP by β- and γ-secretases, respectively, are indicated by arrows. The γ-secretase cleavages are heterogeneous, mainly producing Aβ peptides of 40 and 42 amino acids. The amino acid sequences of Aβ and around the scissile bonds are indicated by the one letter code for amino acids. The sequence shown is the wild-type sequence.

13

Table 1: Potential strategies to inhibit β-secretase processing of APP by BACE-1

No	R_1	R_2	IC_{50} (µM)	pIC_{50}	ΔG (kcal/mol)
	R_1-$C(k)$-[Sta]-Val-R_2				
1*	(structure)	-Ala-Glu-Phe	130	3.89	−15.26
2	(structure)	-Ala-Glu-Phe	140	3.85	−15.41
3	(structure)	-Ala-Glu-Phe	17	4.77	−16.65
4	(structure)	-Ala-Glu-Phe	56	4.25	−15.30
5	(structure)	-Ala-Glu-Phe	42	4.38	−17.26
6	(structure)	-Ala-Glu-Phe	94	4.03	−17.08
7	(structure)	-Ala-Glu-Phe	50	4.30	−15.38
8*	(structure)	-Ala-Glu-Phe	25	4.60	−15.30
9	(structure)	-Ala-Glu-Phe	48	4.32	−16.84
10	(structure)	-Ala-Glu-Phe	28	4.55	−16.79
11	(structure)	-Ala-Glu-Phe	27	4.57	−15.83
12	(structure)	-Ala-Glu-Phe	28	4.55	−15.57
13	(structure)	-Ala-Glu-Phe	41	4.39	−17.34

#	Structure	R	value	value	value
14		-Ala-Glu-Phe	14	4.85	−16.61
15		-Ala-Glu-Phe	6	5.22	−17.37
16		-Ala-Glu-Phe	11	4.96	−15.58
17		-Ala-Glu-Phe	3	5.52	−17.56
18		-Ala-Glu-Phe	4	5.40	−18.20
19*			40	4.44	−17.24
20			50	4.30	−15.21
21			3	5.52	−18.09
22			140	3.85	−16.67

R_1-Val-Met-[Sta]-Val-R_2

#	R_1	R_2	value	value	value
23	Ac–	-Ala-Glu-Phe	0.3	6.52	−20.83
24	(CH$_3$)$_3$COOC–	OH	94	4.03	−15.47
25	(CH$_3$)$_3$COOC–		47	4.33	−17.16
26	(CH$_3$)$_3$COOC–		17	4.77	−16.89
27	(CH$_3$)$_3$COOC–		30	4.52	−17.17
28*	(CH$_3$)$_3$COOC–		4	5.40	−19.87

29	$(CH_3)_3COOC-$		4	5.40	−18.64
30	$(CH_3)_3COOC-$		5	5.30	−18.79
31	$(CH_3)_3COOC-$		0.3	6.52	−19.90
32	$(CH_3)_3COOC-$		10	5.00	−19.13

IDENTIFICATION OF THE β -SECRETASE:

The protein responsible for the activity of β-secretase was reported almost simultaneously by a number of independent groups using quite distinct methodologies. It is unique in being a transmembrane aspartic protease of type I topology, in which the N-terminus and catalytic site reside on the lumenal or extracellular side of the membrane. It has variously been named by different groups as 'β-site APP cleaving enzyme' (BACE), 'aspartyl protease-2' (Asp-2) or 'membrane-anchored aspartic proteinase of the pepsin family-2' (memapsin-2). Vassar et al. originally used an expression cloning strategy to identify genes that altered Aβ production in human embryonic kidney (HEK) cells over-expressing APP containing the amyloidogenic Swedish mutation. This cell line was known to express both the β- and γ-secretases. They isolated a sequence from a clone that produced elevated levels of Aβ and that encoded a novel aspartic protease, which they termed 'BACE' (subsequently BACE-1). A classical biochemical strategy involving affinity chromatographic isolation of the enzyme activity and its subsequent cloning also proved to be highly effective. In another approach, β-secretase was independently identified using expressed sequence tag (EST) databases. Hussain et al. screened a proprietary EST database, from which they identified a sequence of interest which they termed Asp-2. Subsequently, they cloned the cDNA, transfected it into HEK cells and observed an increase in the β-cleavage of APP. From the human EST database at the time, Lin et al. identified, and subsequently cloned and expressed, two novel human aspartic proteinases which they named memapsin-1 and memapsin-2. All groups succeeded in identifying the same protein as the putative β-secretase (BACE-1, Asp-2, memapsin-2), together with a close homologue (BACE-2, Asp-1, memapsin-1). The localization, specificity and other enzymological properties of BACE-1 most closely fitted the profile of β-secretase. Although BACE-2 is interesting in comparative terms, its precise physiological roles are unclear, and there is no compelling evidence that it plays a direct role in the β-secretase processing of APP. Although, inhibitor development studies must clearly consider compound discrimination between the two activities (21).

DEVELOPING B-SECRETASE INHIBITORS FOR TREATMENT OF ALZHEIMER'S DISEASE:

β-Secretase is an important protease in the pathogenesis of Alzheimer's disease. Some statine-based peptidomimetics show inhibitory activities to the β-secretase. To explore the inhibitory mechanism, molecular docking and three-dimensional quantitative structure–activity relationship (3D-QSAR) studies on these analogues were performed. The predictive abilities of these models were validated by some compounds that were not included in the training set. Furthermore, the 3D-QSAR models were mapped back to the binding site of the β-secretase, to get a better understanding of vital interactions between the statine-based peptidomimetics and the protease. Therefore, the final 3D-QSAR models and the information of the inhibitor–enzyme interaction would be useful in developing new drug leads against Alzheimer's disease.

As shown in Table 1, most of the statine based peptidomimetic inhibitors are very long structures and are too hydrophilic, resulting in difficulties in penetrating the blood–brain barrier (BBB). Thus, further structure based drug design study is needed to discover new statine-based peptidomimetic inhibitors that are more drug-like and more active. To the best of our knowledge, neither crystal structures of statine-based inhibitors in complex with neither the β-secretase nor a 3D QSAR model are available.

It has been found that the cerebral deposition of a 40–42- residue β-amyloid peptide (Aβ) is an early and critical feature in AD, indicating a key role of Aβ in the pathogenesis of AD. Accordingly, a hypothesis was proposed that overproduction of the 42-aminoacid form of Aβ might lead to the increased aggregation and deposition of Aβ as a senile plaques in the brain. Aβ is generated from the endoproteolytic processing of the amyloid precursor protein (APP), which is a type I membrane protein with 770 amino acids in length. Firstly, the β-secretase cleaves APP to generate the N-terminus of Aβ, and then, the c-secretase cleaves APP to generate the C-terminus, leading to release of the Aβ. It was followed that preventing the bioactivity of the β-secretase could be therapeutically useful in the treatment of AD. The β-secretase, also known as BACE (β-site APP-cleaving enzyme), which is the protease responding the β-site APP-cleaving, was independently identified by several laboratories using different approaches in 1999. The identification of the β-secretase as BACE provided a target for novel therapies for Alzheimer's disease (22).

DIBENZOTHIAZOLES AS NOVEL AMYLOID-IMAGING AGENTS:

Novel dibenzothiazole derivatives were synthesized and evaluated as amyloid-imaging agents. In vitro quantitative binding studies using AD brain tissue homogenates showed that the dibenzothiazole derivatives displayed high binding affinities with K (i) values in the nanomolar range (6.8-36 nM). These derivatives are relatively lipophilic with partition coefficients (logP oct) in the range of 1.25-3.05. Preliminary structure-activity relationship studies indicated dibenzothiazole derivatives bearing electron-donating groups exhibited higher binding affinities than those bearing electron-withdrawing groups. A lead compound was selected for its high binding affinity and radio-labeled with [(125)I] through direct radio-iodination using sodium [(125)I] iodide in the presence of Chloramine T. The radioligand (4-[2,6']dibenzothiazolyl-2'-yl-2-[(125)I]-phenylamine) displayed moderate lipophilicity (logP oct, 2.70), very good brain uptake (3.71+/-0.63% ID/g at 2 min after iv injection in mice), and rapid washout from normal brains (0.78% and 0.43% ID/g at 30 and 60 min, respectively). These studies indicated that lipophilic dibenzothiazole derivatives represent a promising pharmacophore for the development of novel amyloid-imaging agents for potential application in Alzheimer's disease and related neurodegenerative disorders (23).

LEAD IDENTIFICATION OF ACETYLCHOLINESTERASE INHIBITORS-HISTAMINE H3 RECEPTOR ANTAGONISTS FROM MOLECULAR MODELING:

Currently, the only clinically effective treatment for Alzheimer's disease (AD) is the use of acetylcholinesterase (AChE) inhibitors. These inhibitors have limited efficacy in that they only treat the symptoms and not the disease itself. Additionally, they often have unpleasant side effects. Here we consider the viability of a single molecule having the actions of both an AChE inhibitor and histamine H(3) receptor antagonist. Both histamine H(3) receptor antagonists and AChE inhibitors improve and augment cholinergic neurotransmission in the cortex. However, whereas an AChE inhibitor will impart its effect everywhere, a histamine H(3) antagonist will raise acetylcholine levels mostly in the brain as its mode of action will primarily be on the central nervous system. Therefore, the combination of both activities in a single molecule could be advantageous. Indeed, studies suggest an appropriate dual-acting compound may offer the desired therapeutic effect with fewer unpleasant side effects [CNS Drugs2004, 18, 827]. Further, recent studies indicate the peripheral anionic site (PAS) of AChE interacts with the β-amyloid (βA) peptide. Consequently, a molecule capable of disrupting this interaction may have a significant impact on the production of or the aggregation of βA. This may result in slowing down the progression of the disease rather than only treating the symptoms as current therapies do. Here, we detail how the use of the available crystal structure information, pharmacophore modeling and docking (automated, manual, classical, and QM/MM) lead to the identification of an AChE inhibitor-histamine H(3) receptor antagonist. Further, based on our models we speculate that this dual-acting compound may interact with the PAS. Such a dual-acting compound may be able to affect the pathology of AD in addition to providing symptomatic relief (24).

FLAVONOLS AND FLAVONES AS BACE-1 INHIBITORS: STRUCTURE-ACTIVITY RELATIONSHIP IN CELL-FREE, CELL-BASED AND IN SILICO STUDIES REVEALS NOVEL PHARMACOPHORE FEATURES:

Generation and accumulation of the amyloid β-peptide (Aβ) following proteolytic processing of the amyloid precursor protein (APP) by BACE-1 (β-site APP Cleaving Enzyme-1, β-secretase) and γ-secretase is a main causal factor of Alzheimer's disease (AD). Consequently, inhibition of BACE-1, a rate-limiting enzyme in the production of Aβ, is an attractive therapeutic approach for the treatment of AD. In this study, we discovered that natural flavonoids act as non-peptidic BACE-1 inhibitors and potently inhibit BACE-1 activity and reduce the level of secreted Aβ in primary cortical neurons. In addition, we demonstrated the calculated docking poses of flavonoids to BACE-1 and revealed the interactions of flavonoids with the BACE-1 catalytic center. We firstly revealed novel pharmacophore features of flavonoids by using cell-free, cell-based and in silico docking studies. These results contribute to the development of new BACE-1 inhibitors for the treatment of AD (25).

ALZHEIMER'S THERAPEUTICS: NEUROTROPHIN DOMAIN SMALL MOLECULE MIMETICS:

Factors limiting the therapeutic application of neurotrophins to neurodegenerative diseases include poor stability and CNS penetration. Moreover, certain neurotrophin effects, such as promotion of neuronal death via interaction with the p75NTR receptor, might further limit their application. The development of small molecule mimetics of neurotrophins might serve to overcome these limitations. The proof-of-principle that mimetics of specific nerve growth factor (NGF) domains could prevent neuronal death was already established. Peptidomimetics of the loop 1 domain prevent death via p75NTR-dependent signaling and peptidomimetics of the loop 4 domain prevent death via Trk-related signaling. Screening of *in silico* databases containing non-peptide, small molecules has identified a number of candidate NGF domain mimetics (26).

MATERIALS

The tools used were:

- **ChemDraw**
- **Discovery Studio 2.1**

CHEMDRAW:

ChemDraw is a software program used by chemists worldwide to draw molecular structures (27). It was developed by Cambridge Soft. Chemical structure drawing software is specialized in the chemical structure information with regards to processing, storing, rendering and editing. With the advent of bioinformatics and cheminformatics explosion, professional chemical informatics software for personal computers developed rapidly. For the complexity and speciality of chemical information, to use general-purpose drawing software in chemical structure drawing was painstaking and inefficient. Chemdraw is the most chemical drawing member of the well-known commercial chemical software suite ChemOffice (28).

DISCOVERY STUDIO:

Discovery Studio is a single unified, easy-to-use, graphical interface for powerful drug design and protein modeling research. Discovery Studio contains both established gold-standard applications (e.g., Catalyst, MODELER, CHARMm, etc.,) with years of proven published results, as well as and cutting-edge science to address today's drug discovery challenges. Discovery Studio is built on the Pipeline Pilot Enterprise Server™ operating platform, allowing seamless integration of protein modeling, pharmacophore analysis, and structure-based design, as well as third-party applications (29).

Discovery Studio is been used to:

- Investigate and test hypotheses in *silico* prior to costly experimental implementation, thus reducing the time and expense involved in bringing products to market
- Drive scientific exploration from target identification to lead optimization with a wealth of trusted life science modeling and simulation tools

21

- Leverage an open and scalable platform to automate processes, create and deploy custom workflows, and integrate data types, databases, and third-party or in-house tools
- Enhance personal productivity and boost team collaboration by enabling researchers to share data and make better informed decisions (30).

METHODOLOGY

QUANTITATIVE   STRUCTURE–ACTIVITY   RELATIONSHIP models (**QSAR** models) are regression or classification models used in the chemical and biological sciences and engineering. Like other regression models, QSAR regression models relate a set of "predictor" variables (X) to the potency of the response variable (Y), while classification QSAR models relate the predictor variables to a categorical value of the response variable.

In QSAR modeling, the predictors consist of physico-chemical properties or theoretical molecular descriptors of chemicals; the QSAR response-variable could be a biological activity of the chemicals. QSAR models first summarize a supposed relationship between chemical structures and biological activity in a data-set of chemicals. Second, QSAR models predict the activities of new chemicals (31, 32).

EVALUATION OF THE QUALITY OF QSAR MODELS:

QSAR modeling produces predictive models derived from application of statistical tools correlating biological activity (including desirable therapeutic effect and undesirable side effects) or physico-chemical properties in QSPR models of chemicals (drugs/toxicants/environmental pollutants) with descriptors representative of molecular structure or properties. QSARs are being applied in many disciplines, for example: risk assessment, toxicity prediction, and regulatory decisions in addition to drug discovery and lead optimization. Obtaining a good quality QSAR model depends on many factors, such as the quality of input data, the choice of descriptors and statistical methods for modeling and for validation. Any QSAR modeling should ultimately lead to statistically robust and predictive models capable of making accurate and reliable predictions of the modeled response of new compounds.

For validation of QSAR models, usually various strategies are adopted:

(i) internal validation or cross-validation (actually, while extracting data, cross validation is a measure of model robustness, the more a model is robust (higher q2) the less data extraction perturb the original model);

(ii) external validation by splitting the available data set into training set for model development and prediction set for model predictivity check;

(iii) blind external validation by application of model on new external data and

(iv) data randomization or Y-scrambling for verifying the absence of chance correlation between the response and the modeling descriptors.

The success of any QSAR model depends on accuracy of the input data, selection of appropriate descriptors and statistical tools, and most importantly validation of the developed model. Validation is the process by which the reliability and relevance of a procedure are established for a specific purpose; for QSAR models validation must be mainly for robustness, prediction performances and applicability domain (AD) of the models. Some validation methodologies can be problematic. Different aspects of validation of QSAR models that need attention includes methods of selection of training set compounds, setting training set size and impact of variable selection for training set models for determining the quality of prediction. Development of novel validation parameters for judging quality of QSAR models is also important (33).

DEVELOPMENT OF QSAR MODEL

The construction of QSAR model typically comprises of two main steps: (i) description of molecular structure and (ii) multivariate analysis for correlating molecular descriptors with observed activities/properties. An essential preliminary step in model development is data understanding. Intermediate steps that are also crucial for successful development of such QSAR models include data pre processing and statistical evaluation. A schematic representation of the QSAR process is illustrated in Figure 2.

DATA UNDERSTANDING:

Data understanding is a crucial step that one should not overlook as it helps the researcher to become familiar with the nature of the data prior to actual QSAR model construction thereby reducing unnecessary errors or labors that would otherwise occur. An added benefit is that such preliminary observations can often lead to the identification of interesting associations or relationships to study. However, before exploring the data it is essential that thorough literature search on relevant background information pertaining to the biological or chemical system of interest is performed. This can be achieved through what is known as exploratory data analysis which often starts with simple observation of the data matrix particularly the variables (also known as attributes or fields), its corresponding data types, and the data samples (also called records).

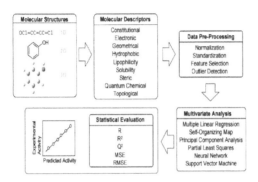

Fig.2: Schematic overview of the QSAR process (Ref: 33)

SELECTION OF TRAINING AND TEST SET:

QSAR models are used increasingly to screen chemical databases and/or virtual chemical libraries for potentially bioactive molecules. These developments emphasize the importance of rigorous model validation to ensure that the models have both the ability to explain the variance in the biological activity (internal validation) and also the acceptable predictive power (external validation). For model validation the dataset is required to be divided into training set (for building the QSAR model) and test set (for examining its predictive ability). For any QSAR model, it is of crucial importance that the training set selected to calibrate the model exhibits a well balanced distribution and contains representative molecules.

Following are the methods for division of the dataset into training and test set:

a) Manual Selection: This is done by visualizing the variation in the chemical and biological space of the given dataset.

b) Random Selection : This method creates training and test set by random distribution.

25

c) Sphere Exclusion Method: This is a rational method for creation of training and test set. It ensures that the points in the both the sets are uniformly distributed with respect to chemical and biological space.

Others : Experimental Design: full factorial, fractional factorial etc., Onion Design, Cluster Analysis, Principal Component Analysis, Self Organizing Maps (SOM) (13).

PHARMACOPHORE:

A pharmacophore is an abstract description of molecular features which are necessary for molecular recognition of a ligand by a biological macromolecule. A pharmacophore model explains how structurally diverse ligands can bind to a common receptor site. Furthermore pharmacophore models can be used to identify through de novo design or virtual screening novel ligands that will bind to the same receptor.

MODEL DEVELOPMENT:

The process for developing a pharmacophore model generally involves the following steps:

1. **Select a training set of ligands** – Choose a structurally diverse set of molecules that will be used for developing the pharmacophore model. As a pharmacophore model should be able to discriminate between molecules with and without bioactivity, the set of molecules should include both active and inactive compounds.

2. **Conformational analysis** – Generate a set of low energy conformations that is likely to contain the bioactive conformation for each of the selected molecules.

3. **Molecular superimposition** – Superimpose ("fit") all combinations of the low-energy conformations of the molecules. Similar (bioisosteric) functional groups common to all molecules in the set might be fitted (e.g., phenyl rings or carboxylic acid groups). The set of conformations (one conformation from each active molecule) that results in the best fit is presumed to be the active conformation.

4. **Abstraction** – Transform the superimposed molecules into an abstract representation. For example, superimposed phenyl rings might be referred to more conceptually as an

'aromatic ring' pharmacophore element. Likewise, hydroxy groups could be designated as a 'hydrogen-bond donor/acceptor' pharmacophore element.

5. **Validation** – A pharmacophore model is a *hypothesis* accounting for the observed biological activities of a set of molecules that bind to a common biological target. The model is only valid insofar as it is able to account for differences in biological activity of a range of molecules.

As the biological activities of new molecules become available, the pharmacophore model can be updated to further refine it.

FEATURES:

Typical pharmacophore features include hydrophobic centroids, aromatic rings, hydrogen bond acceptors or donors, cations, and anions. These pharmacophoric points may be located on the ligand itself or may be projected points presumed to be located in the receptor. The features need to match different chemical groups with similar properties, in order to identify novel ligands. Ligand-receptor interactions are typically "polar positive", "polar negative" or "hydrophobic". A well-defined pharmacophore model includes both hydrophobic volumes and hydrogen bond vectors (34).

PHARMACOPHORE MODELING:

Pharmacophore modeling as a process for predicting pharmacophores with common or specific characteristics among compounds. This definition is applied not only to molecular design but to protein—ligand docking simulation and quantitative structure-activity relationships (QSAR) as well. However, pharmacophore modeling without ligand structural alignment information is difficult. Thus, knowledge of protein—ligand structure is useful for predicting pharmacophores.

The fragment molecular orbital (FMO) method employs *ab initio* quantum mechanical calculations for large biomolecules such as protein—ligand complexes. Intermolecular interaction energies typically can be determined on the basis of molecular mechanics. However, this method is not universally applicable to all compounds, because there is a limit to the determination of molecular potentials based on atom type, especially of quantum chemical elements such as π electrons (35).

PHARMACOPHORE GENERATION:

The key features that are responsible for biological function were generated using pharmacophore model generation. The potential ligands with therapeutic background were used for constructing common feature based pharmacophore model. Initially, molecular interaction studies were performed to identify the activities of all compounds (36).

PHARMACOPHORE MODELING:

In combination of virtual screening, pharmacophore modeling has been proved as an effective strategy for lead compound identification. Compared to pharmacophore modeling, 3D-QSAR is also based on 3D-conformers but considers the overall force field around a molecule, instead of focusing on group features in a single region. Typical programs that generate 3D-QSAR models include comparative molecular field analysis (CoMFA), comparative molecular similarity indices analysis (CoMSIA), and phase. The force fields calculated by 3D-QSAR may be steric, electrostatic, hydrophobic, and hydrogen-bond donor and acceptor. Because 3D-QSAR is best used when ligands share the same structural scaffold, it can be applied in lead optimization for rational drug design (37).

PHARMACOPHORE MAPPING:

Pharmacophore mapping is one of the major elements of drug design in the absence of structural data of the target receptor. The tool initially applied to discovery of lead molecules now extends to lead optimization. Pharmacophores can be used as queries for retrieving potential leads from structural databases (lead discovery), for designing molecules with specific desired attributes (lead optimization), and for assessing similarity and diversity of molecules using pharmacophore fingerprints. It can also be used to align molecules based on the 3D arrangement of chemical features or to develop predictive 3D QSAR models (38).

RESULTS AND DISCUSSION

A list of 16 ligands could be seen in the 3D window of Accelrys 2.1

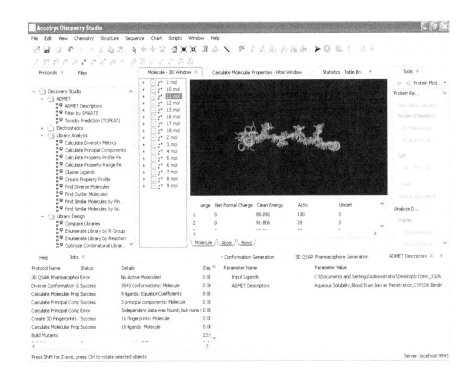

Fig. 3: 16 Ligands in Accelrys Discovery Studio 2.1

MOLECULAR PROPERTIES:

It calculates various molecular properties for ligands. The properties range from traditional molecular descriptors, Semi-empirical QM descriptors, Density Functional QM descriptors and predictions from user models.

Optionally we can:

- Derive a property from other properties (e.g. basic math).
- Generate statistics of numerical properties.
- Tag ligands based on the value of other properties.

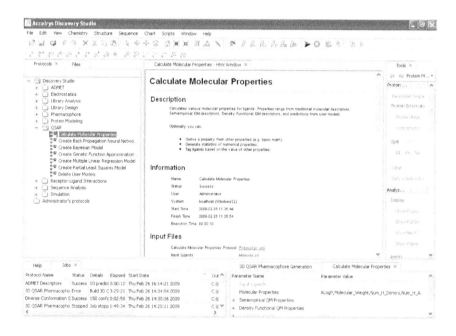

Fig. 4: Screenshot showing calculation of Molecular Properties

The following properties have been identified: ALogP, Molecular Weight, Num_Aromatic Rings, Num_H_Acceptors, Num_H_Donors, Num_Rings, Num_RotatableBonds, Molecular Fractional Polar Surface Area and Molecular Volume.

Table 2 : Statistics Of Molecular Properties

NAME	Mean	Std Dev	N	Min	Max
IC50	46.5	39.9077	16	3	140
ALogP	-1.03744	0.724914	16	-2.42	0.3
Molecular Weight	904.882	29.9665	16	852.028	974.149
Num_Rotatable Bonds	28.1875	1.58976	16	26	32
Num_Rings	2.25	0.559017	16	1	3
Num_Aromatic Rings	2.125	0.599479	16	1	3
Num_H_Acceptors	12.875	0.856957	16	12	15
Num_H_Donors	9.375	0.599479	16	9	11
Molecular_Volume	622.09	22.2304	16	581.04	676.05
Molecular_Fractional Polar Surface Area	0.324698	0.010926	16	0.304066	0.345948

Table 3: Molecular properties of the 16 ligands

S. No	IC 50	ALog P	MW	Num_ Rotat -able Bonds	Num_ Rings	Num_ Arom a -tic Rings	Num_ H_ Accep -tors	Num_ H_ Donors	Mole -cular Volum e	Mole -cular Fraction -al PSA
1	130	-1.315	852.028	27	2	2	12	9	581.04	0.328
2	28	0.3	894.108	28	2	2	12	9	635.23	0.31
3	27	-0.038	910.107	30	2	2	13	9	637.29	0.316
4	28	-1.535	896.08	29	2	2	13	9	619.8	0.321
5	41	-1.656	882.054	27	2	2	13	10	609.51	0.339
6	11	-1.054	974.149	29	3	3	14	11	676.05	0.331
7	3	-1.219	946.923	27	2	2	13	10	616.02	0.333
8	4	-1.059	918.086	27	3	3	13	10	630.43	0.331
9	140	-0.904	888.009	27	2	2	12	9	598.19	0.322
10	17	-1.968	868.027	27	2	2	13	10	594.41	0.346
11	56	0.203	928.124	28	3	3	12	9	640.03	0.304
12	42	-0.407	902.086	27	3	3	12	9	611.56	0.313

13	94	-1.365	942.106	30	2	2	15	9	649.98	0.324
14	50	-2.42	890.074	32	1	1	14	9	622.88	0.337
15	25	-0.945	896.08	30	2	2	13	9	614.65	0.322
16	48	-1.217	890.076	26	3	1	12	9	616.37	0.319

CREATE 3D FINGERPRINTS:

It generates 3 or 4-point pharmacophore fingerprints from ligands or pharmacophores. It identifies all feature locations and enumerates all 3 or 4-point fingerprints according to the binning methods. All conformations of ligands in the input are used. The input can be a 3D database or a pre-calculated set of ligand conformations. Optionally, ligand conformations can be generated. Alternatively, a fingerprint can be identified from an existing pharmacophore.

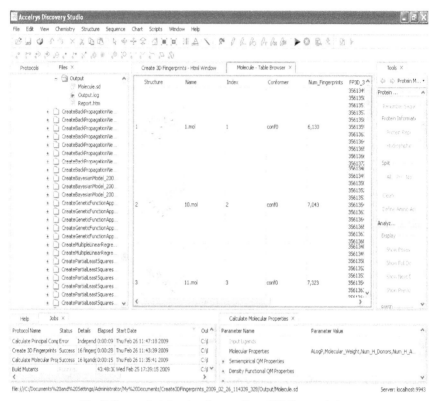

Fig. 5: Screenshot showing the creation of 3D fingerprints

34

STATISTICS OF 3D FINGERPRINTS:

Table 4: Statistics of 3DFingerprints

Name	Index	Conformer	Num_ Finger prints	HB_ ACCEPTOR	HB_DONOR	HYDRO PHOBIC regions
1.MOL	1	conf0	6,130	10	5	5
10.mol	2	conf0	7,043	10	5	6
11.mol	3	conf0	7,323	11	5	7
12.mol	4	conf0	7,142	11	5	5
13.mol	5	conf0	7,282	11	6	5
16.mol	6	conf0	10,393	12	7	6
17.mol	7	conf0	7,974	11	6	6
18.mol	8	conf0	7,422	11	5	5
2.mol	9	conf0	8,237	10	7	5
3.mol	10	conf0	6,841	11	5	6
4.mol	11	conf0	7,221	10	6	6
5.mol	12	conf0	7,111	10	6	8
6.mol	13	conf0	8,672	11	6	4
7.mol	14	conf0	7,015	12	6	5
8.mol	15	conf0	7,071	11	6	6
9.mol	16	conf0	6,879	10	5	6

The fingerprints were stored as an array of "on bits" for each molecule (optionally, each conformation) or pharmacophore. They can be used in any protocol that uses fingerprints. For example: **Create Bayesian Model** and **Find Similar Molecules by Fingerprints**.

CALCULATE PRINCIPAL COMPONENT REGRESSION ANALYSIS FOR 3D-QSAR MODEL GENERATION:

The Principal Component Analysis (PCA) is an orthogonal linear transformation technique that transforms the data into a new coordinate system such that the variance of the data is maximized on the first coordinate (called the first principal component), the rest of the variance maximized on the second coordinate, and so on. The first few principal components can normally explain most of the variance of the data; therefore PCA can be used to reduce the dimension of the data by keeping only the first few principal components.

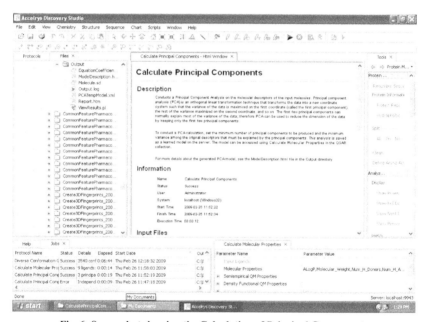

Fig. 6: Screenshot showing the Calculation of Principal Components

To conduct a PCA calculation, minimum number of principal components to be produced was set and the minimum variance among the original descriptors that must be explained by the principal components. This analysis was saved as a learned model on the server. The model can be accessed using **Calculate Molecular Properties** in the QSAR collection.

36

EQUATION COFFICENTS PCA TEMP MODEL:

Table 5: Equation cofficents PCA Temp model

Equation Terms	PCATemp Model_PC1	PCATemp Model_PC2	PCATemp Model_PC3
Constant	18.70348286	-39.89264041	-9.36339
ALogP	0.67623368	-0.101353917	0.38271
Molecular Weight	3.82E-03	1.73E-02	1.22E-02
Num_H_Donors	-0.10422007	0.94448788	-0.51707
Num_H_Acceptors	-0.4333116	0.431172113	0.389986
Num_Rotatable Bonds	-0.18224338	1.43E-02	0.395221
Num_Rings	0.801981735	0.472850893	-0.2817
Num_Aromatic Rings	0.607744974	0.635374238	2.41E-02
Molecular_Fractional Polar Surface Area	-39.597251	21.41027503	-36.8996

This model was built using 16 ligands. It was built with 8 independent variables. The independent properties shown in the table led to a proposed 8 variables for model-building. The properties that were used to provide the variables were: **ALogP**; **Molecular Weight**; **Num_H_Donors**; **Num_H_Acceptors**; **Num_Rotatable Bonds**; **Num_Rings**; **Num_Aromatic Rings**; **Molecular_Fractional Polar Surface Area.**

3D PLOT OF 16 LIGANDS:

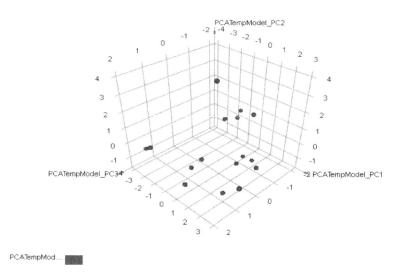

Fig. 7: 3D plot of the 16 ligands

EXTRACTING THE 3D QSAR MODEL:

Various molecular properties for ligands were calculated. Properties range from traditional molecular descriptors, Semi-empirical QM descriptors, Density Functional QM descriptors, and predictions from user models.

Optionally we can:

- Derive a property from other properties (e.g. basic math).
- Generate statistics of numerical properties.
- Tag ligands based on the value of other properties.

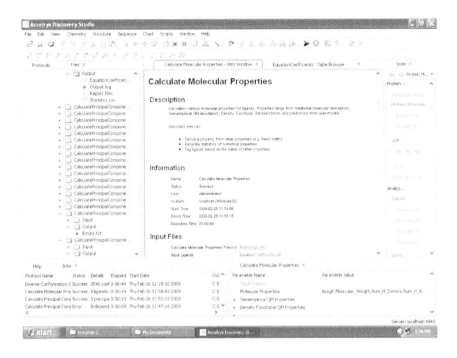

Fig. 8: Screenshot showing calculation of molecular properties

The following properties have been added: ALogP, Molecular_Weight, Num_Aromatic Rings, Num_H_Acceptors, Num_H_Donors, Num_Rings, Num_Rotatable Bonds, Molecular_Fractional Polar Surface Area, PCA Temp Model_PC1, PCA Temp Model_PC2 and PCA Temp Model_PC3.

Table 6: Mean and standard deviation values of the parameters

Name	Mean	Std. Dev	N	Min	Max
Index	5	2.581989	9	1	9
PCATempModel_PC1	-2.16931	14.4419	9	-39.5973	18.7035
PCATempModel_PC2	-1.78536	14.99203	9	-39.8926	21.4103
PCATempModel_PC3	-5.09528	11.62563	9	-36.8996	0.395221
ALogP	0	0	9	0	0
Molecular Weight	0	0	9	0	0
Num_Rotatable Bonds	0	0	9	0	0
Num_Rings	0	0	9	0	0
Num_Aromatic Rings	0	0	9	0	0
Num_H_Acceptors	0	0	9	0	0
Num_H_Donors	0	0	9	0	0
Molecular_Fractional Polar Surface Area	0	0	9	0	0

STATISTICS OF 9 BEST LIGANDS:

Table 7: Statistics of 9 best ligands

EQUATION TERMS	PCA Temp Model_PC1	PCA Temp Model_PC2	PCA Temp Model_PC3
Constant	18.704	39.893	-9.363
ALogP	0.676	-0.101	0.383
Molecular_Weight	0.004	0.017	0.012
Num_H_Donors	-0.104	0.944	-0.517
Num_H_Acceptors	-0.433	0.431	0.39
Num_Rotatable Bonds	-0.182	0.014	0.395
Num_Rings	0.802	0.473	-0.282
Num_Aromatic Rings	0.608	0.635	0.024
Molecular_ Fractional Polar Surface Area	-39.597	21.41	-36.9

ALogP, Molecular_Weight, Num_RotatableBonds, Num_Rings, Num_AromaticRings, Num_H_Acceptors, Num_H_Donors, Molecular_Fractional Polar Surface Area – (Showed Result Zero).

DIVERSE CONFORMATION GENERATION:

It generates diverse conformations of the input ligands. One of the following catalyst algorithms was used:

- **FAST:** quickly provides diverse low-energy conformations.
- **BEST:** ensures the best coverage of conformational space (requires more CPU time).
- **CAESAR:** very quickly provides conformations by sampling torsions.

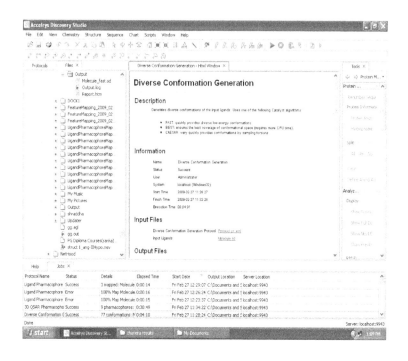

Fig. 9: Screenshot showing Diverse Conformation Generation

42

STATISTICS:

Table 8: Added 5 new conformations to all 16 ligands

Name	Index	Absolute Energy Y	Activ	ConfNumber	Relative Energy	Uncert	Mol. Number
1	1	71.564	130	1	2.477	3	1
1	2	72.81	130	2	3.722	3	1
1	3	69.088	130	3	0	3	1
1	4	75.031	130	4	5.943	3	1
1	5	75.667	130	5	6.579	3	1
10	6	83.1	28	1	3.108	3	2
10	7	79.991	28	2	0	3	2
10	8	94.485	28	3	14.494	3	2
10	9	93.018	28	4	13.026	3	2
10	10	97.084	28	5	17.093	3	2
11	11	90.256	27	1	0.626	3	3
11	12	94.214	27	2	4.585	3	3
11	13	95.905	27	3	6.276	3	3
11	14	96.675	27	4	7.045	3	3
11	15	89.629	27	5	0	3	3
12	16	78.951	28	1	0	3	4
12	17	80.091	28	2	1.14	3	4
12	18	81.334	28	3	2.383	3	4
12	19	84.839	28	4	5.888	3	4
12	20	86.401	28	5	7.45	3	4
13	21	83.196	41	1	0	3	5
13	22	86.535	41	2	3.339	3	5
13	23	89.246	41	3	6.051	3	5
13	24	89.351	41	4	6.156	3	5
13	25	87.709	41	5	4.513	3	5
16	26	103.595	11	1	0.866	3	6

16	27	102.728	11	2	0	3	6
16	28	113.581	11	3	10.852	3	6
16	29	107.675	11	4	4.947	3	6
16	30	111.516	11	5	8.787	3	6
17	31	73.962	3	1	0	3	7
17	32	78.917	3	2	4.955	3	7
17	33	77.11	3	3	3.148	3	7
17	34	74.747	3	4	0.786	3	7
17	35	77.853	3	5	3.891	3	7
18	36	90.993	4	1	0	3	8
18	37	96.731	4	2	5.737	3	8
18	38	96.049	4	3	5.056	3	8
18	39	98.771	4	4	7.777	3	8
18	40	97.377	4	5	6.383	3	8
2	41	71.956	140	1	0	3	9
2	42	73.2	140	2	1.243	3	9
2	43	74.023	140	3	2.067	3	9
2	44	74.69	140	4	2.734	3	9
2	45	73.706	140	5	1.75	3	9
3	46	77.297	17	1	2.244	3	10
3	47	75.053	17	2	0	3	10
3	48	77.171	17	3	2.118	3	10
3	49	76.619	17	4	1.566	3	10
3	50	78.371	17	5	3.318	3	10
4	51	90.377	56	1	0	3	11
4	52	98.954	56	2	8.577	3	11
4	53	99.183	56	3	8.807	3	11
4	54	99.395	56	4	9.019	3	11
4	55	104.429	56	5	14.053	3	11
5	56	90.448	42	1	1.076	3	12

5	57	89.536	42	2	0.164	3	12
5	58	91.715	42	3	2.343	3	12
5	59	89.372	42	4	0	3	12
5	60	97.383	42	5	8.012	3	12
6	61	103.053	94	1	0.922	3	13
6	62	103.644	94	2	1.513	3	13
6	63	102.131	94	3	0	3	13
6	64	103.832	94	4	1.701	3	13
6	65	114.011	94	5	11.88	3	13
7	66	69.054	50	1	0	3	14
7	67	69.477	50	2	0.423	3	14
8	68	77.754	25	1	0	3	15
8	69	79.869	25	2	2.115	3	15
8	70	79.564	25	3	1.81	3	15
8	71	79.149	25	4	1.395	3	15
8	72	84.425	25	5	6.671	3	15
9	73	74.947	48	1	1.262	3	16
9	74	82.708	48	2	9.024	3	16
9	75	83.279	48	3	9.594	3	16
9	76	86.811	48	4	13.127	3	16
9	77	73.684	48	5	0	3	16

3D QSAR PHARMACOPHORE GENERATION:

It generates predictive pharmacophore models from a set of ligands. HypoGen was used to derive Structure Activity Relationship (SAR) pharmacophore models from a set of molecules for which activity values are known.

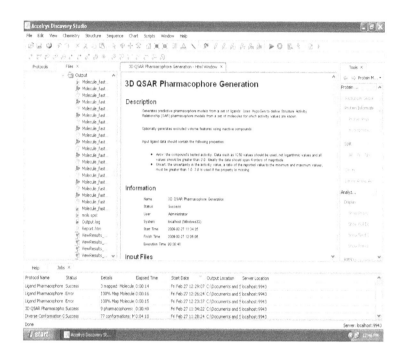

Fig. 10: Screenshot showing 3D QSAR Pharmacophore Generation

46

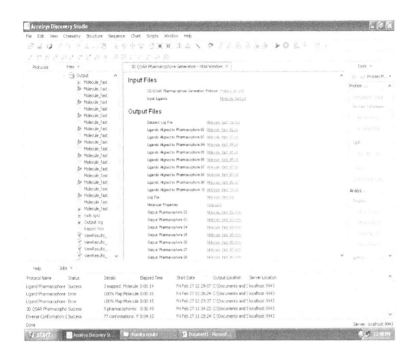

Fig. 11: Screenshot showing Input and Output files

47

HYPOTHESIS BUILD FOR 3D-QSAR PHARMACOPHORE GENERATION:

Input ligand data should contain the following properties:

- Activ: the compound's tested activity. Data such as IC50 values should be used, not logarithmic values and all values should be greater than 0.0. Ideally the data should span 4 orders of magnitude.

- Uncert: the uncertainty in the activity value, a ratio of the reported value to the minimum and maximum values, must be greater than 1.0. 3.0 are used if the property is missing.

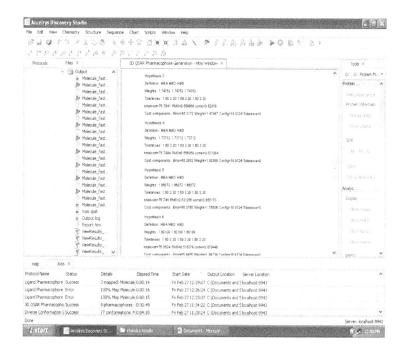

Fig. 12: Screenshot showing the hypothesis (3-6) created by Hypogen

48

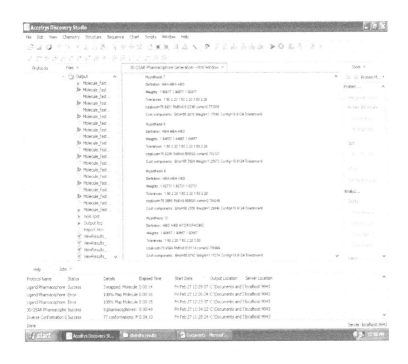

Fig. 13: Screenshot showing the hypothesis(7-10) created by Hypogen

CHM FILE OF PHARMACOPHORE GENERATED:

Hypothesis 9

Definition: HBA, HBA, HBD

Weights are 1.82731, 1.82731, 1.82731

Tolerances: 1.60 2.20 1.60 2.20 1.60 2.20,

Total cost=76.9565 RMS=0.606001 correlation=0.784249, Cost components: Error=56.7556, Weight=1.28848, Config=18.9124 Tolerance=0

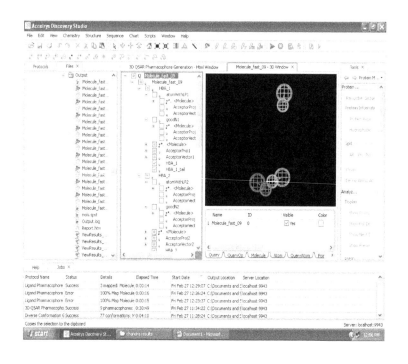

Fig. 14: Screenshot showing Molecule_fast_09

HYPOTHESIS 10

Definition: HBD HBD HYDROPHOBIC

Weights: 1.90667 1.90667 1.90667

Tolerances: 1.60 2.20 1.60 2.20 1.60

Total cost=76.9594 RMS=0.618114 correlation=0.766999

Cost components: Error=56.8742 Weight=1.17274 Config=18.9124 Tolerance=0

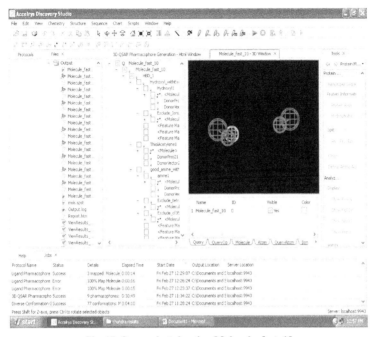

Fig. 15: Screenshot showing Molecule_fast_10

LIGAND PHARMACOPHORE MAPPING:

It maps and aligns the ligands to a pharmacophore. It uses a catalyst to identify ligands that map to a pharmacophore, and aligns the ligands to the query. The pharmacophore can contain combinations of substructures, 3D constraints, features, shapes, excluded volumes, etc., Additional properties may be added depending on the pharmacophore.

51

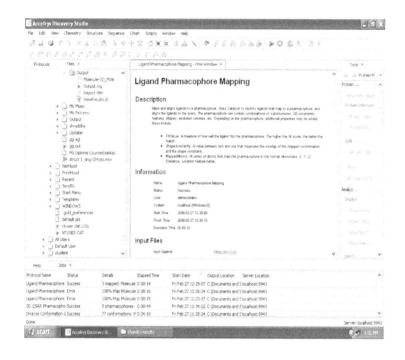

Fig. 16: Screenshot showing Ligand Pharmacophore Mapping

52

3 molecules mapped to the pharmacophore Molecule of 10.chm is shown below.

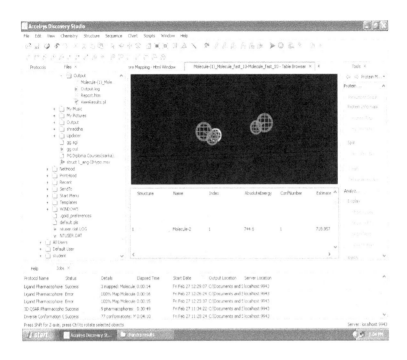

Fig. 17: Screenshot showing pharmacophore Molecule of 10.chm mapping

STATISTICS OF TEST SET:

- **Fit Value**: A measure of how well the ligand fits the pharmacophore. The higher the fit score, the better the match.
- **Shape Similarity**: A value between zero and one that measures the overlap of the mapped conformation and the shape constraint.
- **Mapped Atoms**: An array of atoms that map the pharmacophore in the format Atom Index, X, Y, Z, Tolerance, Location feature name.

Table 10: Statistics of Test Set

S.No	Absolute Energy	Conf No.	Estimate	Fit Value	HBD_1	HBD_2	HYDRO PHOBIC_3	Map No.	Mapped Atoms	Mapping ID	Pharm print	Relative Energy
1	744.6	1	718.957	3.473	1	1	1	1	30,-4.475,-3.535,-5.92,1.6,HBD 1.11 34,7.853,-0.996,2.782,1.6,HBD 2.11	1	'111'	0
2	793.03	1	1236.81	3.238	1	1	1	1	30,-4.475,-3.535,-5.92,1.6,HBD 1.11 34,7.853,-0.996,2.782,1.6,HBD 2.11	1	'111'	0
3	637,499	1	55138	1.589	1	1	1	1	30,-4.475,-3.535,-5.92,1.6,HBD 1.11 35,7.853,-0.996,2.782,1.6,HBD 2.11 27,-3.52,-2.84,-10.24,1.6,Hydrophobic1	1	'111'	0

55

Thus, the 3DQSAR model was build by taking nine best drug from 16 ligands. Pharmacophore features were generated using Accelyrs Discovery Studio 2.1. Finally, a total of nine hypotheses were generated by Hypogen, starting from hypothesis 3 to hypothesis 10. The 10th hypothesis was the best with the total cost value of 76.9594. From the test set, three drugs were mapped to Pharmacophore generated features and out of the three molecules, molecule 2 produced the highest fit value of 3.473 from the test set.

CONCLUSION

A very important part of drug design is the prediction of small molecule binding to a target macromolecule. A reasonable qualitative prediction of binding can be made by specifying the spatial arrangement of a small number of atoms or functional groups. Such arrangement is called Pharmacophore. The Pharmacophore search finds molecules with different overall chemistries, but which have the functional groups in the correct geometry. A common use of Pharmacophore is to search 3D databases for molecules that contain the Pharmacophore.

In this process, 16 structures were designed in ChemDraw (chemoffice) and the compounds were imported in sd and mol file format and displayed in 3D window. Then 3D QSAR model has been generated using Accelrys Discovery Studio 2.1. In this process, molecular properties and 3D finger prints and diverse conformations and ligand pharmacophore features for these structures were calculated.

3D QSAR model was build by taking nine best drugs from 16 ligands. Pharmacophore features were generated. Nine hypotheses were created by hypogen, out of nine hypotheses the last (10th) hypothesis was the best with the total cost value of 76.9594. From the test set, three drugs were mapped to Pharmacophore generated features; out of the three molecules, the molecule 2 which gave the highest fit value of 3.473 from the test set.

Based on the fit value, molecule 2 was concluded to be similar to the training model of 3D QSAR and it could be one of the best drugs for the treatment of Alzheimer's disease.

BIBLIOGRAPHY

1. Alzheimer's Foundation of America. About Alzheimer's disease. AFA Network of Websites
   http://www.alzfdn.org/aboutAlzheimers/definition.html
2. Thorlakur Jonsson, Ph.D., Hreinn Stefansson, Ph.D., Stacy Steinberg, Ph.D., Ingileif Jonsdottir, Ph.D., Palmi V. Jonsson, M.D., Jon Snaedal, M.D., Sigurbjorn Bjornsson, M.D., Johanna Huttenlocher, B.S., Allan I. Levey, M.D., Ph.D., James J. Lah, M.D., Ph.D., Dan Rujescu, M.D., Harald Hampel, M.D., Ina Giegling, Ph.D., Ole A. Andreassen, M.D., Ph.D., Knut Engedal, M.D., Ph.D., Ingun Ulstein, M.D., Ph.D., Srdjan Djurovic, Ph.D., Carla Ibrahim-Verbaas, M.D., Albert Hofman, M.D., Ph.D., M. Arfan Ikram, M.D., Ph.D., Cornelia M van Duijn, Ph.D., Unnur Thorsteinsdottir, Ph.D., Augustine Kong, Ph.D., and Kari Stefansson, M.D., Ph.D. Variant of *TREM2* Associated with the Risk of Alzheimer's Disease. N Engl J Med 2013; 368:107-116. January 10, 2013.
3. Ito N. Clinical aspects of dementia (in Japanese). *Hokkaido Igaku Zasshi.* (May 1996).71 (3): 315–20. PMID 8752526.
4. Alzheimer Europe. Can it be predicted?
   http://www.alzheimer-europe.org/Dementia/Alzheimer-s-disease/Is-there-a-test-that-can-predict-Alzheimer-s-disease
5. Alzheimer's association. Alz.org. Stages of Alzheimer's.
   http://www.alz.org/alzheimers_disease_stages_of_alzheimers.asp
6. Guy M. McKhann. David S. Knopman, Howard Chertkow, Bradley T. Hyman, Clifford R. Jack Jr., Claudia H. Kawas, William E. Klunk, Walter J. Koroshetz, Jennifer J. Manly, Richard Mayeux, Richard C. Mohs, John C. Morris, Martin N. Rossor, Philip Scheltens, Maria C. Carrillo, Bill Thies, Sandra Weintraub, Creighton H. Phelps. The diagnosis of dementia due to Alzheimer's disease: Recommendations from the National Institute on Aging-Alzheimer's Association workgroups on diagnostic guidelines for Alzheimer's disease. Alzheimer's and Dementia The journal of the Alzheimers association
   May 2011. Volume 7, Issue 3, Pages 263–269.

7. Alzheimer's Association Report. 2016 Alzheimer's disease facts and figures. April 2016. Volume 12, Issue 4, Pages 459 – 509.
   http://www.alzheimersanddementia.com/article/S1552-5260(16)00085-6/pdf

8. A. Solomon, F. Mangialasche, E. Richard, S. Andrieu, D. A. Bennett, M. Breteler, L. Fratiglioni, B. Hooshmand, A. S. Khachaturian, L. S. Schneider, I. Skoog, M. Kivipelto. Advances in the prevention of Alzheimer's disease and dementia. Journal of Internal Medicine. Volume 275, Issue 3, March 2014, Pages 229–250

9. Liu A, Guang H, Zhu L, Du G, Lee SM, Wang Y. 3D-QSAR analysis of a new type of acetylcholinesterase inhibitors. Sci China C Life Sci. 2007 Dec;50(6):726-30.

10. Roy KK, Dixit A, Saxena AK. An investigation of structurally diverse carbamates for acetylcholinesterase (AChE) inhibition using 3D-QSAR analysis. J Mol Graph Model. 2008 Sep;27(2):197-208.

11. Alzheimer's society – Drug Treatment for Alzheimer's disease.
    https://www.alzheimers.org.uk/info/20162/drugs/105/drug_treatments_for_alzheimers_disease

12. Marta Nesteruk, Tomasz Nesteruk, Maria Styczyńska, Monika Mandecka, Anna Barczak, Maria Barcikowska. Combined use of biochemical and volumetric biomarkers to assess the risk of conversion of mild cognitive impairment to Alzheimer's disease. *Folia Neuropathol 2016;* 54 (4): 369-374.

13. Quantitative Structure Activity Relationship (QSAR) VLife Sciences Technologies Pvt. Ltd. Pride Purple Coronet, 1st floor, S No. 287, Baner Road, Pune 411 045, INDIA
    http://www.vlifesciences.com/support/Whitepaper/Edusar.pdf

14. Doweyko AM Is QSAR relevant to drug discovery? IDrugs. 2008 Dec;11(12):894-9.

15. Kunal Roy, Supratik Kar, Rudra Narayan Das. Understanding the basics of QSAR for applications in pharmaceutical sciences and risk assessment. Academic Press, 2015 Elsevier

16. G.A. Jicha, E. Abner, F.A. Schmitt, G.E. Cooper, N. Stiles, R. Hamon, S. Carr, C.D. Smith, and W.R. Markesbery. Clinical Features of Mild Cognitive Impairment Differ in the Research and Tertiary Clinic Settings. Dement Geriatr Cogn Disord. 2008; 26(2): 187–192.

17. Tomasz Puzyn, Jerzy Leszczynski, Mark T. Cronin. Recent advances in QSAR studies – Methods and application Challenges and advances in computational chemistry and physics. Springer publications 2010.

18. Recent Advances in QSAR Studies Volume 8 of the series Challenges and Advances in Computational Chemistry and Physics pp 3-11. Date: 30 October 2009

19. Jitender K Malik, Himesh Soni, Singhai A K and Harish Pandey. QSAR - Application in Drug Design. International Journal of Pharmaceutical Research & Allied Sciences. Volume 2, issue 1 (2013), 1-13.

20. Arun K. Ghosh, Margherita Brindisi and Jordan Tang. Developing β-secretase inhibitors for treatment of Alzheimer's disease. J Neurochem. 2012 Jan; 120(Suppl 1): 71–83

21. Clare E. Hunt, Anthony J. Turner. Cell biology, regulation and inhibition of β-secretase (BACE-1). First published: 3 March 2009

22. Zuo Z , Luo X , Zhu W , Shen J , Shen X , Jiang H , Chen K . Molecular docking and 3D-QSAR studies on the binding mechanism of statine-based peptidomimetics with beta-secretase. Bioorganic & Medicinal Chemistry. 2005, 13(6):2121-2131.

23. Wu C, Wei J, Gao K, Wang Y. Dibenzothiazoles as novel amyloid-imaging agents. Bioorganic & Medicinal Chemistry [2007, 15(7):2789-2796]

24. Bembenek SD, Keith JM, Letavic MA, Apodaca R, Barbier AJ, Dvorak L, Aluisio L, Miller KL, Lovenberg TW, Carruthers NI. Lead identification of acetylcholinesterase inhibitors-histamine H3 receptor antagonists from molecular modeling. Bioorg Med Chem. 2008 Mar 15;16(6):2968-73.

25. Shimmyo Y, Kihara T, Akaike A, Niidome T, Sugimoto H. Flavonols and flavones as BACE-1 inhibitors: structure-activity relationship in cell-free, cell-based and in silico studies reveal novel pharmacophore features. Biochim Biophys Acta. 2008 May;1780(5):819-25.

26. Stephen M. Massa, Youmei Xie, Frank M. Longo. Alzheimer's therapeutics. Journal of Molecular Neuroscience. August 2003, Volume 20, Issue 3, pp 323–326

27. Bethany Halford. Reflections On ChemDraw-Recalling the origins of the beloved structure-drawing program as its 30th anniversary approaches. C&EN. Volume 92 Issue 33 | pp. 26-27.

28. Zhenjiang Li , Honggui Wan , Yuhu Shi , and Pingkai Ouyang. Personal Experience with Four Kinds of Chemical Structure Drawing Software: Review on ChemDraw, ChemWindow, ISIS/Draw, and ChemSketch. *J. Chem. Inf. Comput. Sci.*, 2004, *44* (5), pp 1886–1890.

29. Scientific Application – Discovery Studio. The University of North Carolina. http://help.unc.edu/help/scientific-application-discovery-studio/

30. Biovia Discovery Studio. Dassault Systemes. http://accelrys.com/products/collaborative-science/biovia-discovery-studio/

31. R Satpathy and S Ghosh. In-silico Comparative Study and Quantitative Structure-activity Relationship Analysis of Some Structural and Physiochemical Descriptors of Elvitegravir Analogs J Young Pharm. 2011 Jul-Sep; 3(3): 246–249.

32. Quantitative structure–activity relationship. Omics International. http://research.omicsgroup.org/index.php/Quantitative_structure%E2%80%93activity_r elationship

33. Chanin Nantasenamat, Chartchalerm Isarankura-Na-Ayudhya, Thanakorn Naenna, Virapong Prachayasittikul. A Practical Overview Of Quantitative Structure-Activity Relationship. EXCLI Journal 2009; 8:74-88.

34. Pharmacophore. Omics International. http://research.omicsgroup.org/index.php/Pharmacophore

35. Ryunosuke Yoshino, Nobuaki Yasuo, Daniel Ken Inaoka, Yohsuke Hagiwara, Kazuki Ohno, Masaya Orita, *et al.,* Pharmacophore Modeling for Anti-Chagas Drug Design Using the Fragment Molecular Orbital Method PLOS. May 11, 2015.

36. R. Barani Kumar and M. Xavier Suresh Pharmacophore mapping based inhibitor selection and molecular interaction studies for identification of potential drugs on calcium activated potassium channel blockers, tamulotoxin Pharmacogn Mag. 2013 Apr-Jun; 9(34): 89–95.

37. Yongmei Pan, Yanli Wang and Stephen H. Bryant. Pharmacophore and 3D-QSAR Characterization of 6-Arylquinazolin-4-amines as Cdc2-like Kinase 4 (Clk4) and Dual

Specificity Tyrosine-phosphorylation-regulated Kinase 1A (Dyrk1A) Inhibitors J Chem Inf Model. 2013 Apr 22; 53(4): 938–947. Published online 2013 Mar 16.

38. R.A. Hajare, S.T. Landge, V. M. Darvhekar, A.V.Chandewar Pharmacophore in Drug Design and Discovery The Pharma Review (January - February 2011) Kongposh Publications.